MW01171712

manuscript

Magic

Manuscript

Magic

7 Simple Steps to Writing a Book

Heather Davis Desrocher

O'LEARY PUBLISHING
The Influencer's Press

NAPLES, FL

Copyright © 2022 by O'Leary Publishing
All rights reserved.
Published and Printed in the United States
ISBN 978-1-952491-42-9 (paperback)
ISBN 978-1-952491-44-3 (ebook)
Library of Congress Control Number: 2021925630

Ready to be an author?
Schedule Your 30-minute book consultation today.
www.olearypublishing.com

To new authors -
past, present and future.
May you find the
Magic.

Contents

Who Me,
an Author?!

The written word can be transformative, powerful and affirming. Books can help us expand and evolve our understanding of ourselves and the world. They can take us to another time and place while they educate and entertain us. Books can be simply MAGICAL.

One of the joys of being a professional book editor is working with authors who have something meaningful to share. Writers open up and let me into their inner world as we work together to create a book that can change people's lives. I am honored to witness their authentic selves, which often emerge more fully through the writing process.

The written word can also be frustrating and annoying when it is not well done. Some of the headaches of being a professional book editor are correcting the same error over and over in a manuscript or wading through pages of words that are not important in search of the gems that matter and will inspire a reader. Even a tremendous story can end up unread in the Goodwill pile because it is poorly written.

This booklet was born out of the desire to help writers create quality manuscripts and, hopefully, to make the job of editors and aspiring authors easier and more productive.

So what is it that makes a book worth reading? It inspires you; it motivates you;

it entertains you; it educates you; and most importantly, it solves a problem for you. (And, it is error free and easy to read.)

How does an author create a book that does this? That is what *Manuscript Magic* is all about! I am going to pull back the curtain and show you how the magic of creating a book happens. This booklet shares a simple 7-step process that will help you create your book in a way that engages the reader and effectively communicates your message. This is the process that we have refined to help our authors crystallise their manuscripts.

At O'Leary Publishing we know you have a story to tell, and our job is to help you tell it well. When an author comes to us with an idea for a book, we have a 1.5 hour book mapping session with them where we take them through the process outlined in this booklet.

While this is not the only way to write a book, we believe it is the most effective way, and in our experience, it is MAGICAL!

Step

1

Define the Message

In my experience, everyone has a story, but not everyone knows where to start. So, where do you start? You start by defining the message that is uniquely yours to share. The message is the most important part of your book. It drives you to write and shapes what you share.

To create your message, look through your life experiences and determine what you can share that will help others. The lessons you have learned and the wisdom you have gained are valuable and worth sharing. Often your message can come from your greatest challenge or most painful life experience. Your story creates the message that guides your book.

These questions will help you clarify your message: What awareness do you want your reader to have after reading the book? What main life lesson does the book teach?

Here are examples of messages our authors have defined as uniquely theirs:

C. Elliott Haverlack – A life of abundance and fulfillment is available to everyone who seeks it through faith, family and freedom.

Kristina Jay – There are tools and wisdom (or principles) that can guide you through a divorce with dignity, grace and compassion for all involved.

Dr. Paul Arciero – There is a research-supported way to efficiently lose weight, be healthier, and improve performance.

Christine Elwart – There is a map to living with joy and a process to creating the life of your dreams that has been used by some of the most successful people in history.

Dr. Brenda Lyon – There are scientifically proven methods you can use to reduce and eliminate stress in your life.

Valentina Dimitri – When we become aware of our patterns and learn new tools, we can walk the path of transformation to rise above emotional entrapment.

What do you notice about these messages? Hopefully they inspire you and help you to start defining your message. It may be helpful to think of some of your favorite books – ones that made a difference in your life. What was the message of each book? What about them inspired you? Why did that particular author write it? What did they bring to the table that helped them tell their story?

To write *Manuscript Magic* I had to define the message. At first I was developing an acronym and thought the message would be: *P.R.E.P.A.R.E. (Plan, Research, Edit, Punctuate, Audience, Revise, Enjoy)*. But after working with the idea for a while, the message changed. Those were all important tips; but what authors need more is the process, or steps, that one uses to create a book. After some refining, here is the message of *Manuscript Magic*:

There is a magical 7-step process that you can use to create your manuscript.

Of course, there are plenty of other examples you can use to help you define your unique message. To help refine your message, share it with some friends and ask for feedback. Would they read a book with that message? These conversations will help you to further clarify your message.

Take Step 1

Gather a pen and some paper and write down your ideas.

*   What significant experience changed your life?

*   What lessons did you learn?

*   How did the experience change you?

*   What is the universal message that you learned?

*   Are there others who have the same problem who you could help by sharing your story?

Your message will guide you as you continue the creation process and write your book.

Step
2

Identify the Obstacles

There is a metaphysical principle that states: *Once you commit to something, everything that is NOT that shows up.* Once you commit to writing your book and developing your message, the inner critic may start speaking more loudly, reminding you of all the reasons that you cannot (and should not) write.

Most writers (probably all writers) face countless obstacles to writing a book – and I know there are many people who gave up on their dream to write a book because of these obstacles. The good news is you can be prepared to silence that silly little critic when it tells you to quit.

Let's take a look at some of the common lies that may try to prevent you from writing your book. When you hear them, you can laugh and keep writing anyway!

*   I am not an expert.

*   I am not disciplined.

*   I am not influential enough.

*   No one would buy my book.

*   I do not know how to write.

*   I need help to be inspired to write.

*   I am too busy. I don't have the time to write.

*   My voice is not that important. Who do I think I am?

* I am not capable of distilling ideas into cogent written text.

* I am not special. What has happened to me has happened to a lot of people.

* I have all these ideas, but they are all over the place and swirling in my head. They will never amount to anything, anyhow.

What other obstacles can you imagine? Each of the authors with whom I have worked has faced obstacles, but each author persevered to write and publish their book. All of them will tell you that it was worth it!!

Becky Savage, author of *#ONECHOICE: How Ten Seconds Can Change Your Life*, felt that she was not a good writer. She had the added challenge of writing her book in both her own voice and in the voices of her two sons – sons who had both passed from an accidental opioid overdose. With the help of our editorial team and the willingness to do the best she could, her book was published in December 2021, with much fanfare and a #1 New Release status. Everyone we have heard from says how much they enjoyed the book and how grateful they are to have read it. She wrote from the heart and shared a painful story, and this comes through in her words.

Andrew Pierce, author of *Resolving Spiritual Skepticism in Recovery,* works full time as an Addiction Recovery Counselor and plays in a band on the weekends. Time to write was his obstacle; but he was so passionate about his message and how much his book could help others, it fueled him to stay up late writing on a regular basis. His personal experience in recovery has driven him to do whatever he can to pay it forward and help countless others with his book and private practice.

A friend of mine, who is an amazing spiritual teacher, has been trying to write her book for many years; but she becomes bored with writing whenever she works on it. She is a people person and things come to her when she is teaching. Her book comes out of a class that she teaches on masculine and feminine biology and energy. Everyone who takes the class loves it, and all of their relationships improve. For four years, I have pushed her to finish this book – the world needs it! She finally came up with a brilliant solution. She taught the class and had it videotaped. She needed her audience in front of her to "write" her book. Now she can transcribe the video and use the transcripts to help her finish the book. There is always a way!

In writing *Manuscript Magic,* I faced the obstacle of uncertainty. I wrote a complete manuscript over a year ago, called *P.R.E.P.A.R.E. Your Bestselling Manuscript.* I wanted to make sure I included everything that a potential author might need (possibly an impossible goal). This continually kept me from feeling like the book was finished. This is a short book – why was it taking me so long to finish it? Now I realize that the message and focus were not quite right. What helped me overcome my obstacle was when I agreed to be one of the six speakers for our annual BOOKED NAPLES Author-Speaker event. As I worked on my talk, with the help of the other speakers, a better title and format for this booklet was conceived and clarified. It also created a hard deadline for me to finish the book!

As you can see, sometimes we need a creative solution to help us write. Sometimes our messaging switches midstream. Sometimes we need a deadline. Sometimes we need all of these. It is also a good idea to give yourself a proper pep talk and understand that YOU ARE IMPORTANT and YOUR VOICE MATTERS.

Take Step 2

Gather a pen and some paper and write down your ideas.

* What keeps you from writing?

* What doubts do you have about yourself?

* What is your favorite way to share with others (talking, writing, sharing an experience)?

* What part of writing is hardest for you?

* What deadline can you set for yourself to motivate you?

For now, we are going to put the obstacles aside. Once we finish this process, these obstacles will seem much smaller.

Step

3

Clarify the Vision

Once you have defined your message and identified the obstacles, it is time to dream and envision the good that your book can do. In essence you begin at the end – by clarifying your VISION. When your book is published and in your hands, how is it helping the world? What is the book doing for you in your life or business? Clarify in detail why you want to write a book.

There are a wide variety of reasons that a person writes a book. Publishing a book can: leave a legacy for your family; further a mission about which you are passionate; or share expertise that can help others. A book about your business expertise can elevate you in a crowded marketplace and bring higher-value clients. A book with your life stories is valuable to your family, especially once you are no longer here. Experiences that challenge you can give you wisdom, passion or a mission that you are meant to share with others.

Here are seven different visions that compelled our authors to write their books:

1 Sharing An Expertise

The Conscious Divorce: 30 Principles to Help You Choose Yourself by Kristina Jay

Kristina went through a divorce and subsequently wanted to create a handbook with principles that could guide others through the challenging experience of divorce with greater awareness of how to choose themselves. Her own experience gave her wisdom to share.

Resolving Spiritual Skepticism in Recovery: Putting the Universe to Work for You by Andrew Pierce

Andrew, a recovering alcoholic who now works as a counselor helping others in recovery, envisioned a book that would support those struggling with the spiritual aspects suggested in a 12-step program. He saw himself travelling around the country sharing his Unified Theory of Recovery on the radio and in recovery facilities. And that is exactly what he is doing.

2 Telling Your Story

Under a Cloud of Sails: Memoirs of a Free Spirit by Winston Williams

Winston 'Win' Williams came to us at age 84 with a manuscript he had written ten years prior, which he had tried to publish with a traditional publishing company. After receiving no acceptances, the manuscript lay on his shelf – dormant. Through a series of serendipitous events we were able to publish his book, which details both his sailing adventures around the world and his recovery from alcoholism. A unique memoir to be sure. Sadly, Win passed away one year after his book launched. But his story lives on in the pages of his memoir; and his four children, thirteen grandchildren, and two great-grandchildren will treasure his humor and wisdom for years to come.

Great Day…Today! A True Story of Faith, Family, and Football by Bill Kramer

Coach Bill Kramer came to us having just retired from a position as head coach of the Naples High School Football team (1997-2019). Recruited from Miami to Naples in 1997, he and his wife, Sue, moved here with some faith and their three young daughters. Coach Kramer proceeded to transform a losing football program that had very few resources or support into a state champion-ship team in just four years. His book gives readers a front row seat to watch how he did it, and inspires not just football players, fans, and coaches, but also those who are facing obstacles. Endorsed by Dave Wannstedt and Urban Meyer, Coach Kramer shows you that with hard work, faith and God, anything is possible.

3 Educating The Masses

#ONECHOICE: How Ten Seconds Can Change Your Life by Becky Savage

Becky wanted to share the story of losing her sons to an accidental opioid overdose. Her message of primary prevention and education has taken her around the country, speaking widely to schools in order to educate teens about the fatal consequences of drugs and alcohol. Her book and her boys' story is out in the world raising awareness and saving lives.

Haven't You Suffered Enough: Clinically Proven Methods to Conquer Stress
by Brenda Lyon, PhD

Dr. Brenda Lyon worked in the world of academic medicine. For years, she counselled doctors and nurses on the verge of burnout with her clinically proven methods to conquer stress. Then she was diagnosed with cancer. Going through intense treatments, she was able to put her strategies to use and was able to conquer her own stress as her health continued to decline. We were able to publish her manuscript just a few months before she passed. Today, Dr. Lyon is still educating, counselling and helping others through her book. Her work and her expertise live on.

4 Promoting A Passion

Awaken to Unconditional Love: New Wisdom from 20 Spiritual Masters
by Don Fedor, PhD

Don, a retired professor at Georgia Tech, has a unique story to tell. While driven to succeed in the academic world, he simultaneously pursued meditation to cure intense migraine headaches, which lingered from a devastating bike accident. This combination led him into a spiritual quest he never could have expected. In retirement, Don was gifted with messages from 20 Spiritual Masters who asked him to share their wisdom with the world. He was literally compelled to write this book.

5 Leaving A Legacy

From Fear to Fulfillment: A Fight for Faith, Family and Freedom by C. Elliott Haverlack

Elliott has devoted his life to making the world a better place, and wanted to write a book that would awaken the spirit of the American people to rise up and do good. He also wanted to record his amazing life stories and create a guide to abundance for his descendants. His book is not only a gift to his grandchildren, but it is a gift to the world.

An Insubordinate Life: From Country Boy to Candidate for Governor by Loren Culp

Loren Culp's first book *American Cop* opened doors for him that he never could have imagined. This small town police chief ended up running a full-scale political campaign that culminated with him winning a spot on the gubernatorial ticket for the Governor's race in Washington State in November 2020. This year he published his second book, *An Insubordinate Life*, to tell the backstory of who he is and where he came from. It's a book that includes stories and pictures of his time in the Army; lessons learned from owning and running a contractor's business; and his joy as a grandfather that will endear every reader.

6 Growing A Business

Ride the Wave: Journey to Peaceful Living
by April O'Leary

In 2012, April O'Leary was building a Life Coaching practice and found the content she was sharing with private clients was helpful on a larger scale. This book led to the development of an 8-week course that included a workbook and journal. She also launched two conferences and grew her Life Coaching brand. The full story is in *The Influencer's Path to Successful Publishing*.

The Influencer's Path to Successful Publishing by April O'Leary and Heather Desrocher

In 2019, after writing four books, April began O'Leary Publishing to help others publish books. We found that many aspiring authors did not understand the publishing options available to them. This booklet serves a two-fold purpose. It educates a potential client about traditional publishing versus other types of publishing companies. It also showcases our services and helps an author self-select our company with confidence. This tool has helped us generate new business via a free download on our website and has grown our email list.

7 Expressing Creativity

Emanational Expressions: Poems from the Kabbalistic Tree of Life by Alejandro Perez

A busy father and Physician's Assistant, Alejandro also studies Universal Kabbalah. He was inspired to write 11 poems to express his experience and shared them with his classmates. After the class concluded, Alejandro felt it would be beneficial to future students if he published his poems. We were able to help him by adding illustrations to the poems. Now, others who take Kabbalah can use this book to help them on their journey.

Pray Attention: 5 Sacred Meditations with Audio by Rev. Diane Scribner Clevenger

As a Unity Minister, Rev. Diane created a wonderful audio CD of meditations a decade ago. She came to us to create a companion book to help people with dementia access these meditations, and to use as a tool to help children and adults meditate together. We were able to create a beautifully designed book that includes pages for journaling and mandala coloring to guide the reader into a deeper experience.

Which of the seven is closest to your vision for your book? Hopefully these examples give you some ideas and inspiration. Dream a bit. How would a book change your life? How might it change others' lives? Who might benefit from your book?

Take Step 3

Gather a pen and some paper and write down your ideas.

- ★ Do you have a story to tell?

- ★ Do you want to leave a legacy for your family?

- ★ What is your dream? How could a book help with that?

- ★ What could a book do for you or your business?

- ★ How could publishing a book change your life?

- ★ How could your book help others?

Step
4

Imagine the Reader

You have: defined your message; identified the obstacles; and clarified your vision. Now it is time to imagine your reader.

A common problem we see with new manuscripts is an author writing without a clear image of the reader. These manuscripts feel more like journal entries than books that are written to help others. Many first drafts start this way – as a complete brain dump; but to be a manuscript worth publishing, focusing on the reader is the most important thing you can do.

Remember, everyone is tuned into WII-FM – as in, What's In It For Me? If the book is not helping the reader, you can be sure they will not read it. So consider these questions as you outline your target market of readers:

WHO?

Who is reading your book? How old are they? Where do they live? Where do they work? Do they have a family? Are they single? Are they on social media? What television shows do they watch? What do they do for fun? What is their income level? Educational level? Religious background? Nationality? What challenges is this person facing in life?

When you have a clear image of your audience, it is easier to determine what to include in your book and what to leave out.

Here are ways authors have imagined their readers (I will reveal the books at the end of this chapter.):

Reader #1 Someone who wants to write a book but does not know where to start

Reader #2 A child who wants to be entertained and learn about magic

Reader #3 A person who wants to lose weight or have better physical performance and live with optimal health

WHY?

The most important thing to know about your reader is WHY he or she would read your book. What problem does your reader have?

Your answer might look something like these:

Reader #1 Teaches the reader how to start creating a manuscript

Reader #2 Takes the reader on a magical journey of adventure and discovery

Reader #3 Will give the reader the tools to lose weight, be healthier, and improve physical performance

Writing a book, especially a personal one, may bring up deep issues for you. Picturing your reader, and understanding how much your book will help them, can motivate you as you write.

HOW?

It will also be helpful to clarify HOW your book will solve the problem for the reader. Here are some answers to this question:

Reader #1 Offers seven easy steps to map out and begin creating a book

Reader #2 Uses a story to teach children about meditation and the Runes

Reader #3 Uses proven research to create an eating and exercise plan for someone at any level of fitness

As you write, keep your focus on the reader. Periodically ask yourself: WHO is the reader? WHY does the reader care about this? WHAT is a universal theme here? HOW is this a common experience that others have? I suggest to our authors that they write about themes that speak to many people, and keep the focus on the reader.

Put the WHO, WHY and HOW all together, and you have:

Manuscript Magic

This book is for someone who wants to write a book but does not know where to start. It teaches the reader how to start creating a manuscript. It offers seven easy steps to map out and create a book.

Poppy the Awesome Opossum

by Julie LeBriton

This book is for a child who wants to be entertained and learn about magic. It takes the reader on a magical journey of adventure and exploration. It uses a story to teach children about meditation and the Runes.

The PRISE Life: Protein Pacing for Optimal Health and Performance by Dr. Paul Arciero

This book is for a person who wants to lose weight or have better physical performance and live with optimal health. It will give the reader the tools to lose weight, be healthier, and improve physical performance. It uses proven scientific research to create an eating and exercise plan for someone at any level of fitness.

Take Step 4

Gather a pen and some paper and write down your ideas.

* WHO is your reader?

* WHY would they read your book?

* HOW does your book solve their problem?

* Now write it into a three sentence paragraph and see how it feels.

So, you have a message to share. You have a vision for what the book will do for you and for the world. You can see your reader and how the book will help them. Now let's start building your book!

Step
5

Build the Frame

★ ★ ★ ★ ★ ☆ ☆

Writing a book is a bit like building a house: we have already sketched out the ideas on paper – like an architect would – and now we can build the structure or frame.

Your message will serve as the foundation, and the frame is where all your ideas will hang. Building a solid framework will guide your writing and give you a focus.

These questions will help you create the frame for your book:

★ What are the main topics I will discuss?

★ What are the main points I will make?

★ Can they be grouped into categories, parts or sections?

★ How do the topics relate to each other?

★ How do they flow?

Using this information, you can create the Table of Contents for your book. How many chapters will I have? Will they be grouped into parts or sections? Where is the reader when they start this book and where do I want them to be when they finish? What is their experience?

It can be helpful to do this with another person who can ask questions and help you refine what you want to share. Here is a sample table of contents with four parts and 11 chapters that we put together with Valentina Dimitri for her book *Finally Free.*

CONTENTS

Finally Free by Valentina Dimitri

This Table of Contents has a nice balance of four parts with two or three chapters in each part. It also has an interesting theme of the seasons and how they represent our cycles of growth. This invites readers into the book by making them curious to find out more. The Table of Contents may evolve as you write (this one did), but it helps to have one before you start.

Two of our books, *Escaping the Darkness* by Cornell Bunting and *Resolving Spiritual Skepticism in Recovery* by Andrew Pierce, were laid out in two parts. Dividing a book into parts, whether it is two, three or even four parts, can help the reader see the various phases in which you are delivering the material, and gives a nice organizational feel to the presentation. See how these Table of Contents are organized.

CONTENTS

PART II THE LESSONS

Escaping the Darkness by Cornell Bunting

CONTENTS

Resolving Spiritual Skepticism in Recovery by Andrew Pierce

Do these examples give you some ideas for your Table of Contents? What do you like about them? How would yours be different?

Becky Savage's book, *#ONECHOICE*, includes three voices – hers, Nick's and Jack's. Since the timelines overlap when Nick and Jack speak, it made sense to group their stories together based on a timeline. She also included a photo book and a resource section in the back. It is a great combination of personal storytelling and practical information to fully engage her teen reader and leave them with the message that opioids can be fatal – even if you make a choice to use them just one time. Take a look at how this flows:

CONTENTS

#ONECHOICE by Becky Savage

What do you notice about Becky's Table of Contents? What ideas can you take from this example?

Another popular flow for a table of contents is to simply lay out your information chapter by chapter. It does not need to be fancy. Dr. Brenda Lyon's framework is perfect for her book *Haven't You Suffered Enough?* Check it out:

CONTENTS

Haven't You Suffered Enough? by Dr. Brenda Lyon

Let these examples inspire you. Start with your topics and build your framework in the way that best serves your reader and makes sense for the flow of your message.

BONUS: You may also want to create a chapter template to use throughout the book to help you write. Readers like predictability in the layout of individual chapters, so with a framework for each chapter, you can write with ease. Include some (or all) of the following elements:

* Chapter title

* Interesting quotes or questions

* Main point

* Problem the chapter solves for the reader

* Tools the chapter will give the reader

* Stories to include

★ Summary of key points from the chapter

★ Exercises for the reader to do

If you are spreadsheet savvy, I recommend that you create an excel spreadsheet with this information to give you a visual representation of your book. This may evolve as you write, depending on how clear your ideas are for the book; but it is important to give each chapter a structure.

You may also want to create sections within each chapter, each with a section title. This gives readers digestible-sized pieces of information as well as road signs as they read.

Building the framework for your book and for each chapter will help you to create a manuscript that is powerful for the reader and is easy for you to write!

Take Step 5

Gather a pen and some paper and write down your ideas.

★ What are the main topics I will discuss?

★ What are the main points I will make?

★ Can they be grouped into categories, parts or sections?

★ How do the topics relate to each other?

★ How do they flow?

BONUS: Is there a logical format or structure that I can use to make the words flow for the reader inside each chapter?

Step
6

Create the Invitation

★ ★ ★ ★ ★ ★ ☆

At this point you have completed five steps! You have: defined your message; identified the obstacles; clarified your vision; imagined your audience; and written the Table of Contents. Now you are ready to create the invitation into your book. The invitation is just as much for you as it is for the reader. It is your bullseye to help you stay on point as you are writing. It is the short description that will hook the reader into purchasing your book.

How will you invite a reader into your book? Take a few books off your shelf and read the back cover. Does it 'sell' you on what is inside. You purchased that book at some point – do you remember why? Look at the format of a few of the books. Does the flow feel natural? Is there a template approach you can identify? Even though the genres may be different, there is a simple way to write your back cover copy – you do not need to reinvent the wheel. Do what works!

Writing the back cover copy early on helps to refine your book and give you a guiding light as you write. Here is a simple formula for writing the back cover copy for your book:

1. QUOTE

Start with a question, quotation or a bold statement that will catch a reader's attention.

This usually appears at the top center of the back cover.

2. DESCRIPTION

Next, write two paragraphs that highlight the way your book will help the reader. This is not a summary, but rather an invitation. Speak to the readers – tell them what this book will do for them. Include the title (in italics) and your name to make it personal. Share what makes your book compelling, interesting and worth reading.

Again it may be helpful to read the back cover of a few books for inspiration. Pull out your favorite books, go on Amazon, or go to a bookstore and find the section where your book would be found. Read the back covers of a few books to get a feel for what sounds good. What draws you in? What makes you want to read a certain book? Use the ones you like as a model.

Here is a sample of a back cover copy of *Ascend to Joy* by Christine Elwart that invites the reader in, and shares just enough to make someone want to open the book and read more:

Are you ready to experience more joy than you ever thought possible?

If you answered yes, then Ascend to Joy *is for you. Open the pages to discover the secret method to ascend to joy that has been used for thousands of years by some of the wisest, most powerful and successful people in history, like Carl Jung, Nicola Tesla, Michelangelo, and Leonardo Da Vinci, to name a few.*

This method of discovery, also known as Kabbalah, contains a path to the remarkable truth of who you are, and the possibility of who you can become. It is the road map to releasing the scripts of your past and finding your way back to God and to your true self. This book offers you the chance to step out of the confines of life as you have known it, open yourself to limitless possibilities and experience a life of pure joy.

Author C. Elliott Haverlack's book, *From Fear to Fulfillment*, covers a wide array of topics and personal stories. To pull them all together we created the back cover copy that reads as follows:

What if the Impossible Could Become a Reality?

In this world of constant change and a seemingly endless degradation of culture, is it possible to live by faith and not by sight? Is the Bible verse 'with God all things are possible' still as applicable today as when it was written?

In this gripping story, Elliott Haverlack shares his inspiring journey cutting through the weeds of impossibility, sowing the seeds of faith, and ultimately reaping the harvest of what is exceedingly, abundantly, more than he could have ever have expected.

From Fear to Fulfillment *is chocked full of inspiring stories of Faith, Family, and Freedom. Not only will these tales inspire you to believe in the power of God, they will invite you to step out, speak up and stand up for a faith that is so desperately needed in this world today. We live in tumultuous times nearing a dangerous tipping point. We have a country to save. If not us, who? If not now, when? It's a fight worthy of your immediate attention. Say goodbye to fear and hello to fulfilling the work that God has for you to do. Today.*

Police chief and best-selling author Loren Culp's second book, *An Insubordinate Life*, gives his readers a taste of where he came from and who he is today. Here is the invitation into his book, which ends in his own words:

The word insubordinate, defiant of authority, or disobedient to orders, is the antithesis of what Loren Culp is. This book pulls back the curtain and gives you an inside look at the life of one who grew up in rural Washington State and has made a way where, at times, there was no way. Insubordinate? We think not... but we'll let you decide.

A U.S. Army veteran, small business owner, and retired police chief, Loren Culp took his stand to defend the U.S. Constitution in 2018.

He is the author of the #1 best-selling book American Cop, *and in the fall of 2020 set the all-time record for the most votes in Washington State history for a Republican gubernatorial candidate. His stance to protect the citizens from restrictions on their Second Amendment rights and his refusal to mandate masks at his political rallies (because he believes in freedom) gave him and his supporters the label of insubordinate by the current governor. That is when #INSUBORDINATE was born.*

In his own words: "I decided to write this book after about 18 months of campaigning for governor of Washington State and after about 60 years of waking up every morning 'sucking air.' I'm not writing this to say 'look at me' or 'I'm great, read about me.' An Insubordinate Life *is about my life's adventures – some good, some tragic. I hope to show you that it doesn't*

matter who you are or what your background is;
YOU matter and YOU can do anything you set
your mind to. I hope this book inspires YOU, as
YOU have inspired me."

So you can see that writing the back cover
copy of your book does not have to be hard. It
can be a fun way to create an invitation your
potential reader just cannot resist. I bet you
want to buy one of these books now don't you?!

Take Step 6

Gather a pen and some paper and write down your ideas.

Imitation is the highest form of flattery. Read some of the back covers of books on your shelf. Which books speak to you? List the titles. Copy their format and try to describe your message in a few paragraphs that sell your idea to the reader. Tell the reader what they will learn, gain or experience by reading your book. Invite the reader into your book.

Step

7

Find The Team

★ ★ ★ ★ ★ ★ ★

A key to a successful writing and publishing experience is to choose a good team to support and guide you. Think of building a house. How many people does it take to build a house? How many experts in their area? A book is similar. At O'Leary Publishing we have a complete team of vetted professionals to guide you through the process. Appendix II lists and defines each of the people you may want to have on your team.

The person you will likely spend the most time working with is the Developmental Editor, who will coach you through the writing and revision process. This editor will ask lots of questions and make suggestions about how to organize the manuscript.

As an author, you are living and breathing your book, your ideas, your story. An editor's job is to bring a reader's view into the manuscript and find the places that need to be cut, the places that need to be expanded, and to see the writing with a fresh set of eyes. Your editor can see what you cannot. As one of our authors said about the role of a Developmental Editor, "Heather had a wonderful way of holding my hand and kicking my butt at the same time. And it was very effective."

The first draft we write is often for ourselves. We purge all of our thoughts and ideas – and maybe even throw up a little, all over the page. This draft is important because it cleans us out. Once you have released all of this, then you can think and see more clearly. This purge can also uncover what really needs to be said.

So, write a bunch – get it all out – and then go back and sift through draft one to pull out anything that can be used for the real book. Your Developmental Editor will help you with this.

Once you and the Developmental Editor have finished creating and organizing your book, you will work with a Line Editor who will help you with word choice. They will help you improve the tone and flow of the words. Ninety-five percent of really good books were heavily edited just like 95% of model photos are photoshopped! When you receive a manuscript back from the Line Editor and it is marked up with a lot of suggestions, this is a good thing – it means the book will be that much better.

Finally, a proofreader will make sure that your manuscript is error free. The combination of these three different editors helps to create Manuscript Magic!

After the writing and editing phase of book creation, you move on to the design phase, and will work with other members of your team as you move toward your book launch date (more on this in Appendix II).

It is important to know that it takes a team to create a book.

Take Step 7

Gather a pen and some paper and write down your ideas.

If you want to work with someone locally, google 'Book Publishing Company + (your town)' and see what comes up.

OR

Schedule a 30-minute Book Consultation on our website (www.olearypublishing.com/contact-us/) and we can ZOOM with you to talk about your book idea. Many of our authors live thousands of miles away from our headquarters in Naples, FL.

Manuscript
Magic

Now you have the magic formula that many authors use to create a manuscript. I hope that *Manuscript Magic* has shown you how simple it is to begin, and has inspired you to share your message. Now you can use these 7 Simple Steps to create your book:

Step 1 Define the Message

Step 2 Identify the Obstacles

Step 3 Clarify the Vision

Step 4 Imagine the Reader

Step 5 Build the Frame

Step 6 Create the Invitation

Step 7 Find the Team

My wish for you is that you will experience the magic of creating, writing and publishing a book! The world is ready for your message. Ready? Set? Go!!!

Appendix

I

The Parts of a Book

Front Cover

Includes the title, subtitle, author's name, and possibly a graphic or image. Make sure to use the name that is on your website. Hire a professional cover designer – it makes a huge difference. This is the first invitation into your book.

Title Page(s)

Usually two in a row. The first one (half title page) just has the title. The second one also includes the subtitle, the author's name, and the logo of the publisher. These should both be right-facing pages.

Copyright Page

Includes the date of publication, the ISBN numbers, the names of the author, publisher, and the book team (editors, designers, photographer). This is usually a left-facing page.

Dedication (optional)

Usually faces the copyright page and says something like:

> *To my daughter, my heart, may you consciously choose a life of authenticity, empowerment and unconditional love.*

Table of Contents

Lists the parts and chapters of the book and the page numbers. This is a road map to the book. This is generally only used in non-fiction books, unless a fiction book has unique chapter titles.

Foreword

Contains a statement about the book and is usually written by someone other than the author who is an expert or is widely known in the field of the book's topic.

Preface

Invites the reader into the book. It is short and designed to catch the reader's attention. It often shares why the author wrote the book and why a reader would read it.

Front Matter

All of the parts up to this point in this list are part of the front matter, which introduces your book to your readers and sets its tone.

Introduction

Introduces the book and sometimes, additionally, the topic or theme of the book. It usually includes a guide to the layout of the book or how a reader can best use the book.

Afterword (optional)

Places the book into a larger context. May include new information or experiences that have happened since the manuscript was originally written.

Acknowledgments

Thanks those who helped the author in life or with the book. We like this to come at the end of the book as it will have more meaning to the reader after having read the book.

Personal Reflection (optional)

Additional information by the author regarding personal experiences that did not fit in the main body of the book.

Appendix (optional)

Supplemental information for the reader to reference: charts, lists, terms, exercises.

Reading List (optional)

Book recommendations from the author related to the theme or topic of the book.

References (optional)

Lists the sources of information or quotes used by the author in the book.

About the Author

Presents the author and his or her life. Usually includes a summary of relevant degrees and professional experience.

Back Cover (Copy)

Invitation into the book that speaks to the readers and tells them what the book will do for them. This is NOT a summary of the book.

Appendix
II

The Book Team

Author

The person who writes the book about their own experience or knowledge.

Publisher

The company responsible for all aspects of your finished book project.

Ghost Writer

A person who writes a book for another person. This involves interviewing the "author."

Project Manager

The person who oversees the book team and the project. He or she communicates with all of the professionals working on the project

Developmental Editor

Most people have never heard of a Developmental Editor (DE) – they are the secret weapon an author uses to create an awesome book. The DE is like an architect who helps the author to build the structure that houses all the words included in the manuscript. The DE asks a lot of questions to help clarify what the book needs to include. The time a DE works with an author can be weeks, but is more often months.

Line Editor

The second stage of the book editing process is Line Editing. After the author and the

Developmental Editor have finalized the overall structure of the manuscript and the flow of the ideas, the manuscript moves on to the Line Editor. The job of the Line Editor is to review the manuscript sentence by sentence, removing unnecessary words and refining word choice. This process makes the book smoother for the reader. It is a bit like adding in the furniture and decorations to a new house, and hopefully, this stage of editing ends with a beautiful manuscript.

Proofreader

The third, and final, stage of the editing process is Proofreading to find any errors. These errors could be in spelling, grammar or punctuation.

Illustrator

The artist who brings the author's ideas to life in images.

Cover Designer

The professional who designs the cover based on the author's ideas and input. This is a special skill set, and hiring a professional is worth it! He or she will have experience, knowledge and special software to design a professional cover.

Interior Designer

The professional who designs and lays out the interior based on the cover design. This involves a lot more than most people realize to have a book that has a professional-looking interior.

eBook Designer

This person takes the final book design and creates the ebook format that is popular for

Kindle, Nook and other e-reader platforms. The nice thing about ebooks is the text size can be enlarged, the background can be turned to night mode, and the fonts can be changed by the reader. This is a must-have option.

Launch Manager

The launch manager creates the timeline for the launch of your book. They determine, with you, whether or not to offer your book for pre-order, and if so, for how long. They also plan your launch strategy to get the word out about your book to your network, and help coordinate any online or in person event you might desire for the launch of your book.

Publicity Manager

The publicity manager, also known as a publicist, is the person responsible for soliciting earned media spots for you and your book. We work closely with a reputable PR firm and connect our authors that want to pursue media opportunities with them.

Social Media Manager

The social media manager is the person (or team) responsible for content creation and posting on your behalf on your social media platforms. This often includes engagement with other accounts. It is their responsibility to keep up with the current trends and algorithms to help your posts achieve the farthest reach possible, and the most engagement.

About the Author

Heather grew up on a ranch in California and earned degrees in sociology and education from Harvard College where she graduated Magna Cum Laude. During high school and college, Heather taught swimming; and after graduating she became a middle school teacher of English and social studies. Heather loves books – especially in the personal growth and spirituality genres.

For ten years, Heather was a stay-at-home mom, and for six years she was the Director of Religious Exploration at the Unitarian Universalist Congregation of Greater Naples. In 2017, Heather began studying Metaphysics and ancient healing modalities with the Modern Mystery School International, and is passionate about spirituality and magic.

Heather is the Head Editor at O'Leary Publishing, and lives in Naples, FL, with her daughters and their dog, Leo "the little lion."

To find out more about
publishing your manuscript
download our complimentary guide:

The Influencer's Path to Successful Publishing
at www.olearypublishing.com

Made in the USA
Columbia, SC
19 February 2025

53989457R10054